Young Adult Literature

Magical Worlds

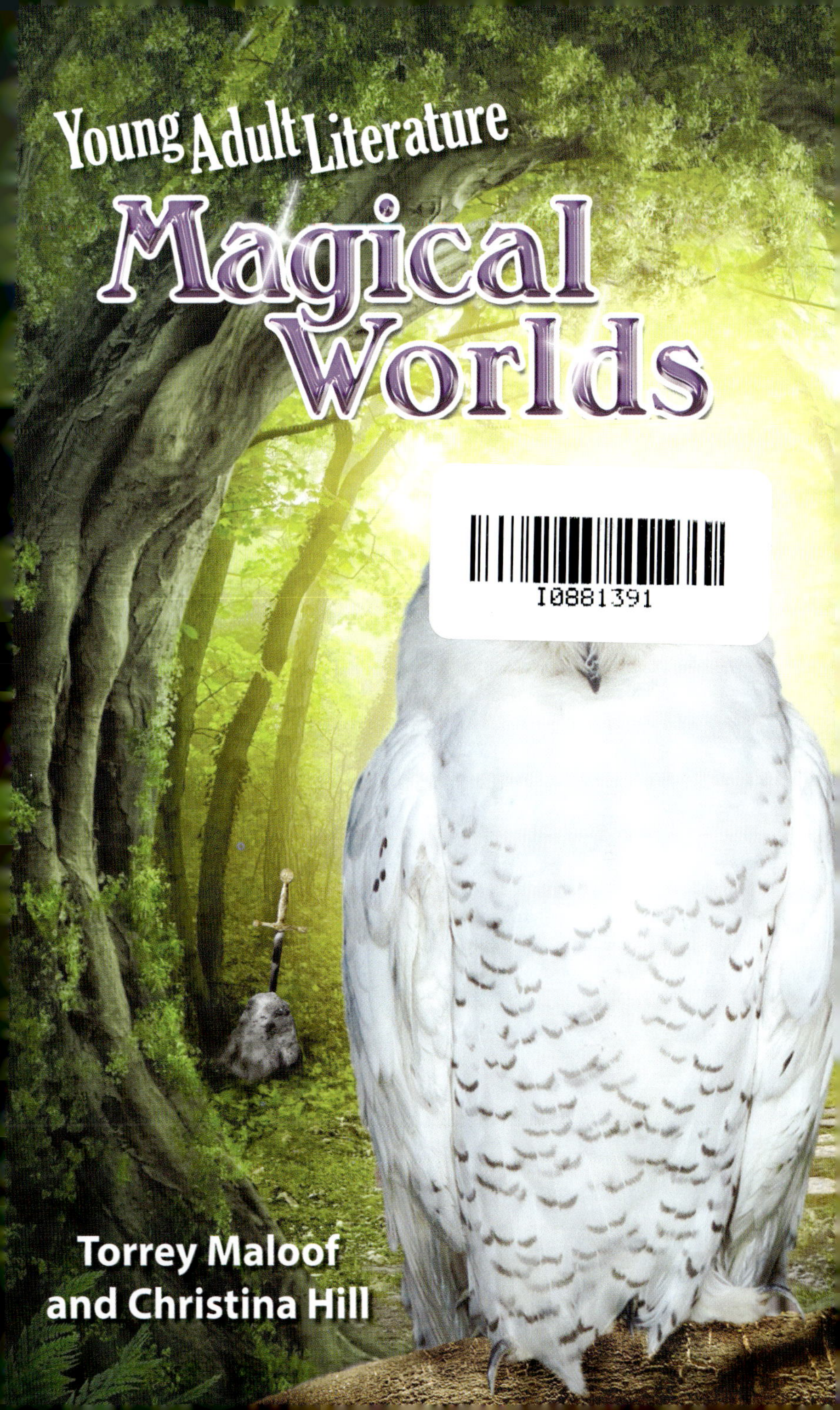

Torrey Maloof
and Christina Hill

Consultants

Timothy Rasinski, Ph.D.
Kent State University

Lori Oczkus, M.A.
Literacy Consultant

Publishing Credits

Rachelle Cracchiolo, M.S.Ed., *Publisher*
Conni Medina, M.A.Ed., *Managing Editor*
Dona Herweck Rice, *Series Developer*
Emily R. Smith, M.A.Ed., *Content Director*
Stephanie Bernard and Susan Daddis, *Editors*
Robin Erickson, *Multimedia Designer*

Image Credits: p.5 Pictorial Press Ltd/Alamy; p.10 (left) INTERFOTO/Alamy, (right) Robin Marchant/Getty Images; p.11 (top) Nomi Ellenson/Getty Images, (bottom) WENN Ltd/Alamy; p.19 Flickr.com/Public Domain; p.21 Moviestore collection Ltd/Alamy; pp.22–23 AF archive/Alamy; pp.24,26 ZUMA Press, Inc./Alamy; p.27 Moviestore collection Ltd/Alamy; All other images from iStock and/or Shutterstock.

Teacher Created Materials
5301 Oceanus Drive
Huntington Beach, CA 92649-1030
http://www.tcmpub.com

ISBN 978-1-4938-3597-3

Made in China.
Nordica.012018.CA21701269

Table of Contents

A Powerful Spell

Why is the magical world so mighty and alluring? How does it cast such a powerful spell over readers? Magical **realms** are exciting and adventurous. They can also feel comforting and strangely familiar. Each story provides an escape from the stresses of everyday life. Reading fantasy novels allows readers to enter unique worlds. These worlds are full of curiosities and enchantments. And yet, even in these mystical realms, there is a sense of familiarity. At their hearts, despite the fantasy settings, these books tell deeply human stories.

Young adult readers connect well with magical worlds. On the surface, these worlds are nothing like their own. But readers see elements of themselves in the magical characters. This is even true when the characters are witches or wizards! Teenagers identify with the struggles and problems the **protagonists** face. They can relate to the challenging circumstances, even if the circumstances involve fighting a monster or flying on a broomstick. Young adults who are facing their own challenges can sink into the characters' worlds. The books may even help them feel as though they are facing their challenges with new friends.

Why is it so easy to connect to these new worlds and characters? Could it simply be . . . magic?

One of the First!

One of the earliest magical realms is Camelot. Many parts of the Camelot stories contain historical facts. This makes some people believe they are real. The line between fantasy and reality often blurs as stories are told over time.

Before CGI technology created Gollum, he lived on the pages of J. R. R. Tolkien's books.

CGI Magic

CGI stands for computer-generated imagery. This technology brings many of the most-loved magical realms and characters in literature to life on the big screen. Of course, all the technology in the world can't hold a candle to your imagination!

There's No Place Like Home

Literary worlds can be magical. Sometimes, these fictional realms are packed full of **innovative** ideas and **mythical** beings. They are like nothing we have ever seen or imagined. Other times, they may resemble our own world at first glance. But the more you read, the more magical elements you find.

These magical realms are powerful blends of fantasy and reality. The young adults who read these stories often find ways to relate them to their own personal journeys. There are often **metaphorical** bridges in these stories that connect the two worlds. What a perfect setting for teens who are making the difficult transition from childhood to adulthood.

What Is Young Adult Literature?

Young adult literature is a genre aimed specifically at teenagers. While fantasy novels make up a good portion of young adult literature, there are many other subcategories to explore, including mystery, historical, dystopian, and contemporary.

Enchanted Escapes

Some magical realms are complete escapes from our world. J. R. R. Tolkien created a large fantasy world for his Lord of the Rings series. His stories take place on a large continent called Middle-earth. The land is full of mythical beings. There are elves, hobbits, and tree-like creatures called ents. The land is detailed and complete. Tolkien even made maps of his magical world!

Magical realms can be set anywhere, from faraway galaxies to **fathoms** below Earth in elaborate underwater kingdoms. No matter the setting, there is imagination, enchantment, and wonder. This is where the power of fantasy stories lies.

To Consider . . .

Authors who create complex magical realms have quite a lot to think about. Here are just a few of the many questions authors must consider when creating their magical worlds.

- What are the rules and laws of this society?
- What are the customs and cultures?
- What is the history of this world?
- What kinds of clothes do the characters wear?
- Are there schools for learning?

The Hidden Magical World

Magical realms are often connected to real-life locations in literary worlds. In stories, the magical world and real world often overlap in unexpected ways. The magic remains hidden and quiet. This entices readers to think that there may be magic surrounding them as well. They just can't see it.

J. K. Rowling's Harry Potter lives in a nonmagical village outside London, England. He is not aware that a magical realm even exists until he is accepted into Hogwarts School of Witchcraft and Wizardry. That is because it is hidden from nonmagical folks, or as Potter fans know them, Muggles.

Crossing the Threshold

Sometimes, protagonists can access magical realms from the ordinary world. Usually, they must cross through some sort of **threshold**. The threshold can be anything that allows entry into the magical realm. It can even be an ordinary object.

- Harry Potter travels to his magical school by a train that he boards from the secret platform 9¾.
- The Pevensie children enter Narnia through what appears to be an ordinary wardrobe.
- Alice first enters Wonderland by a dream and later through a mirror.
- Dorothy enters Oz by being swept up in a tornado.
- Bastian enters the land of Fantastica by reading a story and magically becoming part of the plot!

Isabella "Bella" Swan, from Stephenie Meyer's *Twilight*, lives in the town of Forks, Washington. In that town, teenage vampires and werewolves (or shape-shifters) appear to be normal people. They go to school, date, and fall in love. But the more you read, the more you learn about the hidden world of these mysterious creatures.

This is true in many fantasy stories. As you read, the differences between the ordinary world and the fantasy one become more apparent, even as they are made to feel real through the real-world connections. The more the reader learns, the more real the world becomes. In this way, young readers can connect to these new realms. The reader is lured in through the magical spells they weave.

Frenzy in Forks

After *Twilight* hit the shelves, tourists began **infiltrating** the tiny town of Forks, Washington. The previously quiet community is often swarming with fans who are eager to see the places described in Bella and Edward's world. The visitor center even distributes *Twilight* maps showing places of interest.

DIG DEEPER!

Creating a Magical Realm: How Did They Do That?

Your Mission: Create an entire magical universe using only your imagination. Fun? Yes! Easy? Nope! Magical realms must be places where storylines can unfold naturally and where characters have room to live and grow. A magical realm is so much more than a location. It has to be unique, expansive, detailed, and well thought out. Here's how some of the pros have crafted their magical realms.

1940

1960

Ursula K. Le Guin

Le Guin's most powerful tool for creating fantastical worlds is her imagination. This can be seen in her Earthsea series. She states on her website that most of the research she does is into the "geography of (her) own imagination."

J. R. R. Tolkien

Tolkien stated that long before writing *The Hobbit* and The Lord of the Rings trilogy, he had "constructed this world mythology." He explained that he relied on maps to help construct his complex settings and stories. "If you're going to have a complicated story," he said, "you *must* work to a map; otherwise you can never make a map of it afterwards."

J. K. Rowling

The creator of Harry Potter confessed that she spent five years "constructing The Rules" for her magical world. She said, "I had to lay down all my parameters. The most important thing to decide when you're creating a fantasy world is what the characters *can't* do."

1990

2000

Christopher Paolini

To create the world of Alagaesia when he wrote *Eragon*, Paolini asked himself many questions. "Who might find a dragon egg out in the middle of nowhere? How did the dragon egg get there? Who else might be looking for the dragon egg?" Those questions and others helped him develop an amazing, mystical world.

Magical Sensibility

Magic, a common literary device in fantasy fiction, is often essential to the plots of the stories. What is it about magic that casts spells over young adult readers? What draws them deeper into the stories? Surprisingly, the answer lies in the *reality* of the magical realms. Reading about realms that feel real makes it easier for teens to connect to the stories and characters. It reminds them of their own lives and struggles.

Dragons . . . Again?

Think about dragons. Since they are imaginary, you have obviously never seen one. Yet you can picture one in your mind. Repetition of magical ideas and imagery, like dragons, can help them seem real.

I'm Extraordinary, Too!

Fueled by energy and hormones, young adults can often feel invincible even while struggling with the hectic passage into adulthood. What better way to embrace this crazy time than to visit other worlds? It would be great to wake up one morning in a new, exciting world and be able to morph into something magical!

Making the Unbelievable Believable

One key to writing fantasy is keeping it just real enough to be believable. These stories encourage readers to **embark** on magical journeys. The journeys serve as escapes from the familiarity of the readers' lives. For many young adults, routine days seem to blur into endless repetitions of school, homework, and extracurricular activities.

However, the power of fantasy realms is not just escapism. What makes these novels successful is their **realism**. For instance, Charlie, in Jenny Nimmo's *Midnight for Charlie Bone*, attends a special school. He must go to school, study, and take exams. Despite having magical powers, he and other magical protagonists still struggle with real issues. They may fight with their parents. Or they may have to find dates for school dances. Magic can help with a lot, but it will only get the character so far. Teenage problems remain problems whether the person is magical or not!

Magical Limits

There is a limit to everything, including magical powers. What would happen if magical characters had unending power? There would be no conflict and very little action as a result. Limited power helps create struggles in the stories. These struggles move the stories along. Conflict and struggle also help readers identify with the characters and make them relatable.

Some characters are born with magical gifts. In Rick Riordan's mythological series, Percy Jackson is the son of the mighty god Poseidon. But even he has limitations. He is impulsive and quick to anger. He needs time to develop and grow. But, his limitations help develop the story. He learns that his ADHD and dyslexia are signs of his godliness. As he learns, his magical feats start small. Then, they grow as his journey unfolds.

A Responsible Balance

In Le Guin's *A Wizard of Earthsea*, magic is everywhere. Those who are gifted in the magical arts can study wizardry at a special school. The more they learn, the more powerful they become. However, there are limits. The good wizards focus on remaining in harmony with the world around them. They must learn the consequences of their wizardry and strive to find the right balance between the darkness and the light.

Tools of the Trade

Magical realms often come with some pretty cool tools. From swords and spells to books and broomsticks, these tools can help or hinder the protagonists along their journeys. But the tools also come with rules and limitations. Some tools may only be used by worthy individuals. Others may only be used at certain times. Misusing magical tools may lead to dire consequences.

Amulets/Talismans

These items are small, often **ornate** objects with magical powers. They protect the people who wear them against attacks, but perhaps in limited ways. In the first book of the Bartimaeus trilogy by Jonathan Stroud, an amulet can only block magical assaults. It will not protect the person who wears it from a physical fight or minor injuries, such as a paper cut.

Broomsticks

Forget sweeping the floor, magical broomsticks are built for flying! Broomsticks are one of the better-known magical items. They appear in many magical stories. In *Hex Hall* by Rachel Hawkins, Sophie uses brooms to fly around with other witches.

Invisibility Cloaks

These special cloaks are magical pieces of clothing. When one is worn, it makes the person wearing it invisible to others. These cloaks allow people to hide from enemies, explore forbidden areas, or gain secret information by **eavesdropping**. King Arthur, Frodo, and Harry Potter all have cloaks of invisibility in their **arsenals**.

For Real?

Did you know the U.S. military and other scientific researchers are working on ways to make objects invisible? They are attempting to cover objects in special ceramic coatings. The objects would not physically disappear, but they would blend in with their surroundings. They would even be undetectable using radar.

Potions

There is a potion for almost every problem. Some potions heal sickness and wounds, like Lucy's cordial in C. S. Lewis's *The Lion, the Witch and the Wardrobe*. Others transform people's appearances. There are potions that provide magical powers. Other potions can conjure evil forces, and of course, there are love potions. Remember, though, many potions have side effects.

Rings

Magic rings can offer protection, immortality, or invisibility. But they can also be cursed and dangerous. Perhaps the most **infamous** magic ring is the One Ring from the Lord of the Rings trilogy. Sauron put so much of his dark power into the ring that he couldn't survive without it. The One Ring is able to control the other rings of power dispersed throughout Middle-Earth.

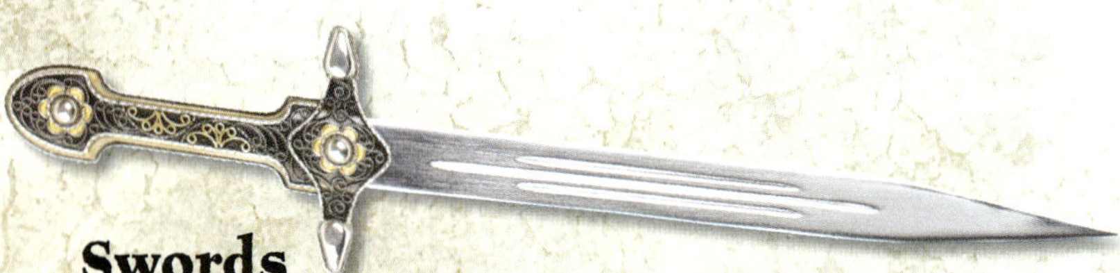

Swords

Magical swords are more than just weapons of steel. They sometimes help people perform tasks. They might even have special powers. In T. H. White's *The Sword in the Stone*, Arthur is the only one worthy of pulling the sword, Excalibur, from the stone. This magical sword later helps him perform great deeds throughout his reign.

Wands

Wands are usually depicted as long, thin tools. They are typically made from the wood of sacred trees. In T. H. White's The Once and Future King series, Merlyn carries a wand made from an exotic and sturdy wood. Other wands may be made of precious metals. C. S. Lewis's White Witch from Narnia uses a wand made of gold. Wands are used for a variety of things. They may cast spells, fight off enemies, or even partake in magical duels.

STOP! THINK...

Look closely at the first cover of *Peter Pan* (originally titled *Peter and Wendy*) by J. M. Barrie. Use the image to answer the questions.

- What details does this cover show?
- What magical elements does this cover include?
- What can you infer about this book from the cover?

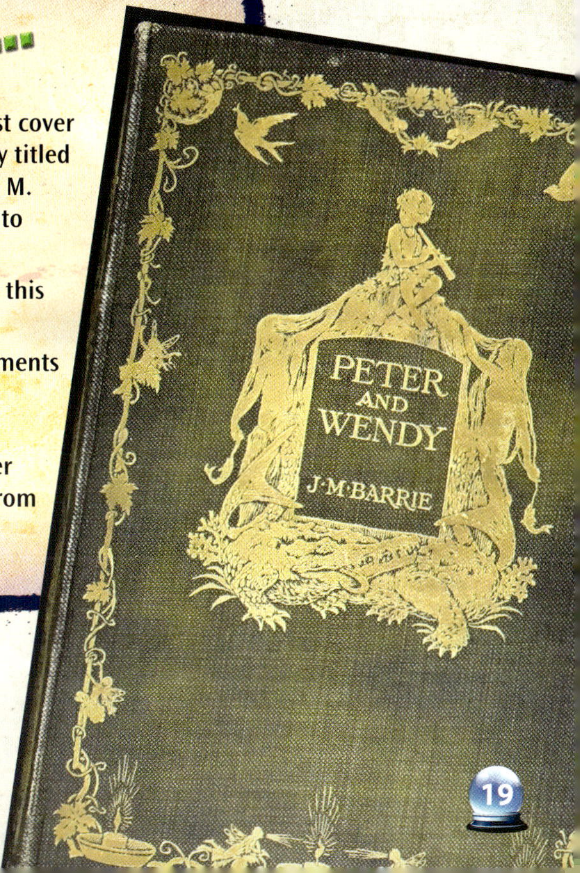

The "Magic" of Friendship

Supporting characters are essential to good literature. These characters are often close friends of the protagonists. The friendships among the characters help make the stories realistic. This is another way fantasy tales cast their magical spells over readers. Friendships are key to making these tales relatable. After all, nobody relies on his or her friends more than teens do!

I'll Be There for You

Percy Jackson has many supportive friends that help him in his journey. One loyal friend is Grover Underwood. He remains by Percy's side, even when Percy makes questionable choices. An empathy link between the two allows them to communicate through unspoken emotions or even in dreams.

Some friendships form at the beginnings of stories. The bonds that tie the characters together never break. Readers may long for this kind of deep friendship. This model of devotion is something we all hope to find. It helps create a feeling of belonging.

Friends Until the End

In Tolkien's Lord of the Rings trilogy, Frodo decides to take a long journey. His best friend, Sam, pledges to help him and to remain by his side. Their **alliance** is tested along the way. But their friendship supports them throughout their journey and evolves as the plot moves forward.

Frodo and Sam

Finding Friends at Last

Some protagonists begin their journeys as outsiders or loners. They may be the new kids at school. Or they might be the only humans in a magical realm. Many young adult readers can identify with the anxiety of being new kids. They can also understand feeling alone. Teenagers may feel alone even when they're in the middle of a crowd.

Furry Friend

In *The Neverending Story*, Atreyu and Falkor, a luckdragon, work together to save the realm of Fantastica from "The Nothing" that eats away at its very existence. Atreyu triumphs with the help of this amazing friend.

Atreyu and Falkor the luckdragon from *The Neverending Story* filmed in 1984

Lonely characters usually find friends along the way. These friends become the loyal companions who see the protagonists through their quests. In *Artemis Fowl* by Eoin Colfer, Artemis is a loner whose only real friend is his bodyguard. He fights an entire world of underground magical creatures. Later, one of the fairies, Holly Short, works with him to fight evil forces.

Steadfast Animal Companions

Sometimes, the most trustworthy friends are animals. This is especially true in magical realms. Magical creatures often serve as faithful sidekicks. They are always ready to lend helping hands (or paws, or wings). Animals can sometimes be more reliable than people. For some characters, it is easier to whisper fears and frustrations to furry friends.

The Wise Teacher

Most heroes in young adult fantasy literature are teenagers themselves. While teens may think they know everything, there is certainly more to learn. This is especially true in magical realms! Cue the wise teachers. These characters act as guides to help shape and **mentor** the younger characters on their quests for magical greatness.

Follow in my Footsteps

Many times, magical mentors are parental figures to the young protagonists. Brom trains Eragon in combat fighting, magic, and the art of the Dragon Riders. Brom's own experiences help him impart wisdom and knowledge to Eragon.

Eragon and Brom as depicted in the 2006 film

Protective Mentors

Magical mentors are typically older and wiser than the main characters. They can also serve as protective guides to help keep the protagonists safe. While these mentors are extremely powerful, they are usually only there to impart wisdom. The final battles against evil are up to the young protagonists.

But, not all mentors are much older than the main characters. In Kristin Cashore's novel, *Graceling*, Po is only a couple of years older than the protagonist. This does not stop him from being a helpful and wise mentor though. He encourages Katsa to find out the truth about who she is. He also helps her recognize how much power she has.

Glinda's Secret

In L. Frank Baum's *The Wonderful Wizard of Oz*, Glinda, the Good Witch of the North, is Dorothy's magical mentor. She gives Dorothy a gift—a pair of silver shoes. These shoes have the power to get Dorothy home to Kansas. However, Glinda does not tell Dorothy about the shoes' magical power until her journey in Oz is complete!

Choose the Right Path

Wise teachers do more than teach magic and provide protection. They also offer the protagonists codes of conduct to follow. These codes are based on **morality**. They are reminders that good triumphs over evil. If the heroes choose wisely, they will successfully conquer their obstacles.

Lion-hearted Peter

Aslan in *The Lion, the Witch and the Wardrobe* is a strong mentor for all the Pevensie children, but especially for Peter. As Peter begins his journey to becoming king, Aslan helps him discover his bravery.

In White's *The Sword in the Stone*, Merlyn uses magic to turn Arthur into different animals. Although humorous, these changes serve as lessons for Arthur. Each lesson lies in the experience itself! For example, when Arthur is a fish, he learns that he can use his wit to defeat a stronger enemy. In each situation, Arthur acquires wisdom. These experiences help shape Arthur's character as he grows up and remind him to choose the right path once he becomes king.

May the Force Be with You

The timeless fascination with George Lucas's Star Wars movies inspires many authors to pen stories in this galaxy. In Tom Taylor's *Luke Skywalker and the Treasure of the Dragonsnakes*, Luke's magical mentor is Yoda. According to Yoda, fear, anger, and hate all lead down the wrong path. He teaches Luke to focus his thoughts and energy on the good side of the Force.

DIG DEEPER!

The Magical Realm Checklist

The more fantasy literature you read, the more you notice certain elements that appear over and over again. How many books have you read that have wizards? Have you read more than one book that includes a magical sword? The next time you read a book about a magical realm, see which items on this list you can locate. You can even use this checklist to help you create your own magical realm.

Animals

- ☐ cat
- ☐ dog
- ☐ horse
- ☐ mouse
- ☐ owl
- ☐ snake
- ☐ spider

Magical Tools

- ☐ amulet
- ☐ book
- ☐ broomstick
- ☐ car
- ☐ carpet
- ☐ cloak
- ☐ elixir
- ☐ hat
- ☐ potion
- ☐ ring
- ☐ spell
- ☐ sword
- ☐ talisman
- ☐ wand

Creatures

- ☐ centaur
- ☐ dragon
- ☐ elf
- ☐ fairy
- ☐ giant
- ☐ goblin
- ☐ hobbit
- ☐ ogre
- ☐ Pegasus
- ☐ phoenix
- ☐ sea serpent
- ☐ troll
- ☐ unicorn

Supernatural Characters

- ☐ shape-shifter
- ☐ sorcerer
- ☐ vampire
- ☐ warlock
- ☐ werewolf
- ☐ witch
- ☐ wizard

Other

- ☐ seed
- ☐ tree

The Classic Conflict

The common literary **theme** of good versus evil is **prevalent** in many young adult fantasy tales. This timeless struggle helps draw readers into the story. That is because the conflict is relevant to all people, even in nonmagical worlds. Teenagers especially can face difficult choices every day. At times, making the right choice can feel like choosing between good and evil. It may seem like an easy decision to make, but that's not always the case. The dark side can be enticing! And, darkness can be deceiving. It may be difficult to tell who or what represents evil.

The Power of Darkness

Evil is always powerful. Dark lords are characters who have chosen to sacrifice good in favor of evil. Typically, these characters begin with good intentions and later experience some sort of a fall from grace. This leads them to the dark side. As they embrace the darkness, their identities change.

A New Name = A New Identity

When characters choose the dark side, they often form new identities. Sometimes, they are cursed with new names. Other times, changing their names is their choice. They hope that by choosing new, intimidating names, people will begin to fear them and their powers.

- In the Harry Potter series, Tom Riddle becomes obsessed with rejecting his Muggle family name. He changes his name to Lord Voldemort.
- In the Star Wars saga, Anakin Skywalker chooses the dark side and is reborn as the Sith Lord Darth Vader.

The Triumph of Goodness

Characters are often torn between choosing good or evil. This internal struggle is relatable to the real world. The moral of these fantasy stories is that **virtue** and goodness reign. In the end, the protagonist wins by choosing the right path and conquering the evil darkness or the villain.

Le Guin's Earthsea series is a great example of an internal struggle of good versus evil. Tenar is a priestess who lives underground. She is surrounded by darkness and the evil influence of the Nameless Ones. She is meant to assist in the execution of Ged, the hero. But when he arrives, she struggles to carry out the task. His kindness convinces her to spare him. Through much **turmoil** and internal struggle, she eventually sees the peace found in goodness. Ultimately, Tenar leaves the darkness behind and follows Ged into the outside world.

A Blend of Both

Gregory Maguire's *Wicked: The Life and Times of the Wicked Witch of the West* puts a clever spin on characters from *The Wonderful Wizard of Oz*. Maguire challenges the definitive good versus evil battle between the Wicked Witch and Glinda the Good Witch. He blurs the lines between good and evil to prove a point. We all are capable of good and evil.

The Journey

Most stories follow similar patterns. First, the setting and characters are described in detail. The plot moves forward, leading up to the major conflict. The **climax** of the story occurs when the action reaches a turning point. Then, the protagonist solves the problem. The story ends with a **resolution**.

All protagonists embark on some sort of journey as they move through this story pattern. The journeys may be literal voyages or internal journeys of self-discovery. Don't be fooled by the simple plot pattern! Fantasy stories often have many twists and turns. There may be countless conflicts along the way. Magical realms are **unpredictable**. That's one way to keep readers turning the pages!

The Saga Continues

Many fantasy novels are written as multiple books. There are six books in the Mortal Instruments series. There are four books in the Twilight series. It took eight books to finish Charlie Bone's story. And the stories of Oz include a whopping 40 books! But why is this? Fantasy realms are complicated. Because they differ from our world, it is important that they are described in great detail. Plus, these books appeal to huge numbers of readers who plead for more!

The Ultimate Boon

In his classic writings, including *The Power of Myth*, author Joseph Campbell describes the hero's journey well. He also shows how sometimes heroes are in search of items that will help resolve the conflicts that generated their journeys. They can only receive these boons, or vital items, once they have proven themselves worthy. This means they have to endure many **trials** and challenges before achieving success.

The Literal Quest

In some tales, the main characters' journeys begin in their homelands. Yet when the conflicts arise, the heroes must leave home in search of solutions. The journeys may be to obtain magical items. The characters might have to defeat evil wizards. Or they might need to rescue friends in trouble. Heroes might pass through magical forests, explore underwater kingdoms, or cross into new time dimensions. The beauty of the quest is learning more about the magical realms. And the excitement of the journeys lies in the adventures found along the way.

In Peter Beagle's *The Last Unicorn,* the Unicorn's journey follows this pattern. She leaves her forest on a quest to find other unicorns. She is afraid she may be the last of her kind. Along the way, she has magical encounters. She faces difficult obstacles. She also meets many unique characters. The heroine may be a magical unicorn, but her struggle to understand love and to find others like herself is a familiar **theme**. It is one to which many young adult readers can relate.

Who Am I?

At times, magical characters must go on journeys to discover who they really are. Laurel is the protagonist in Aprilynne Pike's *Wings*. One morning, she wakes up to find a huge flower blooming on her back. The journey she takes allows her to discover her true self among the faerie world hidden from humans' prying eyes.

A Journey through Space

In Madeline L'Engle's *A Wrinkle in Time*, Meg goes on a search through time and space to find her father. Along the way, she encounters many strange creatures and mysterious forces. This literal journey eventually takes Meg to other planets to fight against dark forces.

Self-Discovery

Most protagonists in young adult literature are teenagers. As their stories progress, they often age into early adulthood. This transitional time is tricky for the characters as well as for young readers. Emotions are heightened. Many experiences are first ones—first date, first love, first job. The protagonists are trying to figure out who they are. But through this time, teenagers gain independence and prepare to enter the real world. This theme of self-discovery also exists in the fantasy realm. Luckily, most fantasy characters have magic to aid them in their coming-of-age journeys.

In the Twilight series, Bella Swan is an average, awkward junior in high school. She is the "new girl" in school. In this way, many readers can relate to Bella. When Bella meets Edward (who happens to be a vampire!), she falls in love for the first time. Her journey is filled with drama, danger, and heartbreak. Yet, these experiences are what help her grow. They help her **mature** emotionally. Bella's quest is one of self-discovery.

What's Your Spirit Animal?

In Philip Pullman's *The Golden Compass*, each character has a daemon—an animal or creature that represents one's soul. Daemons are constantly shifting into different animals. This is because the characters are on journeys of self-discovery. Eventually, after the characters reach adulthood, daemons settle into specific animals that best represent the characters' personalities.

DIG DEEPER!

Magic Mountain Map

It doesn't matter who is in the story, where it takes place, or what it's about—stories in magical realms typically follow a similar pattern. The map is a framework to help you navigate the next magical story you read.

Going Up?

The action starts to build as the story unfolds. The protagonist faces conflicts and the excitement increases.

In the Beginning ...

Here's where we meet our protagonist. We get to know the who, what, and where of the story. The why and how of the magic is just starting to unfold.

The Summit!

This is the climax of the story—often the most exciting part! It is where the action shifts and the protagonist faces the core challenge head-on.

Going Down?

The protagonist solves the problem and resolves the conflict during this time. The hero is happy again!

In the End ...

At this point, the protagonist has learned something valuable and grown as a person. The story is nicely wrapped up, but the reader may wish for more as he or she faces the end of a great book.

What's the Magic Word?

There are so many enchanting and alluring elements at the center of magical realms. They all work together to create powerful, magical spells. These spells capture the readers' attention and take them along on journeys of discovery. At the end of those journeys, teenage readers are rewarded with deeper understandings of themselves and the world in which they live. They have been on long, sometimes grueling adventures with characters who might feel like good friends. Young adult readers may feel as though this journey has helped them through their own problems.

Readers come away from these stories with their own sets of "magical" tools that they can use. Those tools may be different for every reader. One may come away with more self-confidence. Another reader may harbor more courage. Still another may find validation. Each and every young adult's experience is different; however, most readers will agree that the journeys are definitely worth taking. So, when it comes to these books, what do you suppose is the magic word? Well, maybe it's two words: More, please!

Beyond Books

Books that take us to magical realms have become so popular that they have spawned blockbuster movie franchises. But that's not all. They've also inspired action figures, video games, landmarks, and even theme parks!

The Millennium Bridge in London is destroyed by Death Eaters in the film version of *Harry Potter and the Half-Blood Prince.*

THINK LINK

- How does a reader know that he or she is entering a magical realm?
- What purpose do magical tools serve in fantasy fiction?
- In what ways does life in a magical realm resemble life in the real world?

Glossary

alliance—a union formed to help both sides

arsenals—collections of weapons

climax—the most intense point in a story; before the resolution

eavesdropping—secretly listening in on other people's conversations

embark—to begin a journey

fathoms—units of length used to measure the depth of water

infamous—being well known for bad reasons

infiltrating—passing through

innovative—introducing new methods or ideas

mature—showing the emotional and mental qualities of an adult

mentor—a faithful and wise teacher or advisor

metaphorical—a figure of speech in which a word or a phrase is used in place of another to show similarity between them

morality—beliefs about what behavior is right or wrong

mythical—existing only in the imagination

ornate—decorative or fancy, usually with patterns and shapes

prevalent—accepted or common

protagonists—important main characters in stories who make good choices

realism—a style of art or literature that shows or describes people and things as they are in real life

realms—communities, territories, or kingdoms

resolution—the act of finding a solution to a conflict

theme—the core subject or message of a piece of writing

threshold—the point of entering or beginning

trials—tests of someone's ability to do or endure something

turmoil—a state of confusion, agitation, or commotion

unpredictable—incapable of being known before it happens

virtue—a good or moral quality

Index

Check It Out!

Listed below are the series and books from this reader as well as others you may be interested in checking out!

Baum, L. Frank—The Wizard of Oz series

Beagle, Peter S.—*The Last Unicorn*

Buckley, Michael—The Fairy Tale Detectives (The Sisters Grimm) series

Carroll, Lewis—Alice's Adventures in Wonderland series

Cashore, Krisitin—*Graceling*

Chainani, Soman—The School for Good and Evil series

Clare, Cassandra—Mortal Instruments series

Colfer, Chris—The Land of Stories series

Colfer, Eoin—Artemis Fowl series

Funke, Cornelia—The Inkheart trilogy

Le Guin, Ursula K.—Earthsea Cycle series

Levine, Gail Carson—*Ella Enchanted*

Lewis, C. S.—Chronicles of Narnia series

Maguire, Gregory—*Wicked: The Life and Times of the Wicked Witch of the West*

Meyer, Stephenie—Twilight series

Mull, Brandon—Fablehaven series

Nimmo, Jenny—Charlie Bone series

Paolini, Christopher—Inheritance Cycle series

Pike, Aprilynne—Wings series

Pullman, Philip—*The Golden Compass*

Riordan, Rick—Percy Jackson and the Olympians series

Rowling, J. K.— Harry Potter series

Steward, Trenton Lee—The Mysterioius Benedict Society series

Tolkien, J. R. R.—The Lord of the Rings series

White, T. H.—The Once and Future King series

Try It!

As an up-and-coming new author, you've been contracted by a publishing company to create an original story that's set in a magical realm. What kind of world will you invent? Refer to the checklist on pages 28–29 as you complete these steps.

- Draw a map of your magical world to share the setting. Make sure to include a key of important landforms, landmarks, and any other secrets your world might hold.
- How does the protagonist discover the magic in his or her world?
- What magical tools will be used?
- Who will be the antagonist? A person? An animal? A fictional beast? Draw a picture of this character.
- Describe the major conflict for the protagonist. What obstacles will be faced by the protagonist in the story?
- How will the book's conflicts be resolved?

About the Authors

Torrey Maloof and Christina Hill have been BFFs for years and have much in common. They share a love of reading and consider Jane Austen to be their "wise teacher." They can often be found basking in the sun on a Southern California beach or with their noses buried in books at a local bookstore. Christina enjoys spending time with her husband and two young sons, who are all *Star Wars* fanatics. Torrey loves chasing after her young niece who loves all things Disney. The two friends love looking for the magical elements that exist in the real and hectic world in which they live.

Table of Contents

Magic, Imagination, and Science

Step right up, folks, gather 'round. Have we got a treat for you! Illustrious **illusions** will intrigue your imaginations. Stupendous scenes of **sleight of hand** are right around the corner!

Marvel at the mystifying and mesmerizing **mentalist**. Transfix your eyes on terrific **transformations** and **teleportations.** Let legendary **levitations** lift your mind and spirit. Witness fantastic physical feats that fool the senses and boggle the mind.

Healing Magic

The Karanga people of Zimbabwe believe that **supernatural** forces can cause sickness. They use herbs and perform rituals to treat the illnesses. The rituals are said to unleash magical properties in the herbs. This, in turn, heals the patient.

The Magic of Myth and Legend

A prince flies a magic carpet high above an Arabian desert. A wizard places a sword inside solid stone. A magician folds a lake in half to find a lost amulet. Stories of great magic have been a part of almost every culture for thousands of years. But why? What is our collective fascination with magic? And is magic real or just myth and legend?

The Magician's Oath

The secrets behind magic tricks and illusions are closely guarded. In fact, magicians even swear an oath to prevent non-magicians from knowing how they create their magical acts.

"As a magician I promise never to reveal the secret of any illusion to a non-magician, unless that one swears to uphold the Magician,s Oath in turn. I promise never to perform any illusion for any non-magician without first practicing the effect until I can perform it well enough to maintain the illusion of magic."

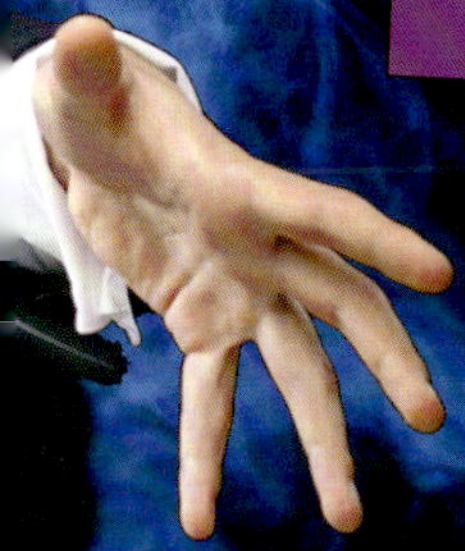

Our Limited Senses

Science is the study of our universe. We explore and experiment. We make observations and catalog our understandings. Our five senses help us understand what we observe. But there are things that we cannot observe with our senses. Scientific tools can help us expand our senses. Even with tools and invention, our understanding is limited.

Imagine you took your smartphone back in time to medieval England. The people of that time may look at the smartphone with fear and amazement. You may find yourself running for your life as they try to destroy the smartphone and you along with it! To them, your smartphone is magical and even supernatural.

Fooling Our Senses with Science

Magician Doug Henning was known to say, "The magic of today is the science of tomorrow!" Magicians through the ages have studied the limits of human senses. The illusions they perform work outside the range of those senses. Using science and technology, magicians and illusionists are able to fool our senses.

Career Spotlight—Illusion Designer

Magicians need a team of experts to help them craft large illusions. Do you want to make an elephant disappear or teleport across the room? Illusion designers are there to help. They use advanced algebra and geometry to affect the audience's perspective. They also design and build props and help the magician perform the illusions.

The Power of a Story

It's not enough for a magician to create the props needed to perform an illusion. A magician also needs to lead the audience's attention. Through story and **patter**, or dialogue, an illusionist leads you to believe one thing while showing you another.

Doug Henning

You Can't Believe Your Eyes

When it comes to illusions, you really cannot trust your eyes. A magician who has mastered illusion can make things appear and disappear at will. A magician can transform a man into a tiger or make a zebra's stripes vanish. Illusions bend our perception of reality and show us the amazing, the impossible, and the bizarre!

Lights, Camera, Apparition!

Magicians and illusionists have long used the properties of light to intrigue audiences. Imagine yourself sitting in a dark theater. A magician on the stage waves his arms in large, slow, circular movements. With the muscles in his face tensed, he says a few mysterious magic words in a commanding voice.

HSSSSS! A foggy mist floats across the floor and a shadowy figure materializes, staring straight at the audience! You gasp and almost leap out of your seat. The magician looks on in awe, as shocked as the audience. He has just produced a ghost!

The ghost floats gracefully across the stage, gives one last look at the audience, and vanishes. The audience erupts in applause.

The Proteus Cabinet

The Proteus cabinet is a stage prop that uses mirrors to make people disappear. Inside a cabinet, two mirrors are set at angles against a pole so they reflect the sides of the cabinet. During the illusion, an assistant steps into the cabinet. The doors close, and the assistant hides behind the mirrors. When the cabinet is reopened, the assistant seems to have vanished.

Say the Magic Words

Some magicians say magic words to add mystery to their shows. "Abracadabra" is probably the most famous magic word. In the 1920s and '30s, the great magician, Dante, would say, "Sim sala bim" after performing illusions to draw applause from the audience.

DIG DEEPER!

Pepper's Ghost

How did the magician make the ghastly **specter** emerge from nothingness? The answer has to do with the reflection of light and a man named Dr. John Henry Pepper. Dr. Pepper was the first to adapt this ghostly illusion for stage performances. He used the effect in the 1862 run of Charles Dickens's play *Haunted Man*.

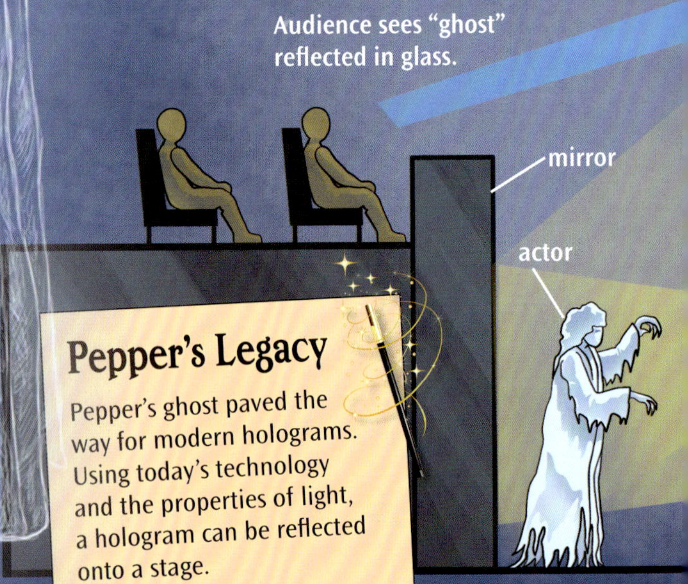

Pepper's Legacy

Pepper's ghost paved the way for modern holograms. Using today's technology and the properties of light, a hologram can be reflected onto a stage.

Setting the Stage

Pepper's ghost may seem like the work of ghoulish magic. But really, the ghost appears because of the properties of light—specifically that light waves can be reflected. Look at the stage design of the Pepper's ghost illusion below. Follow the path of the reflected light to see how this illusion works.

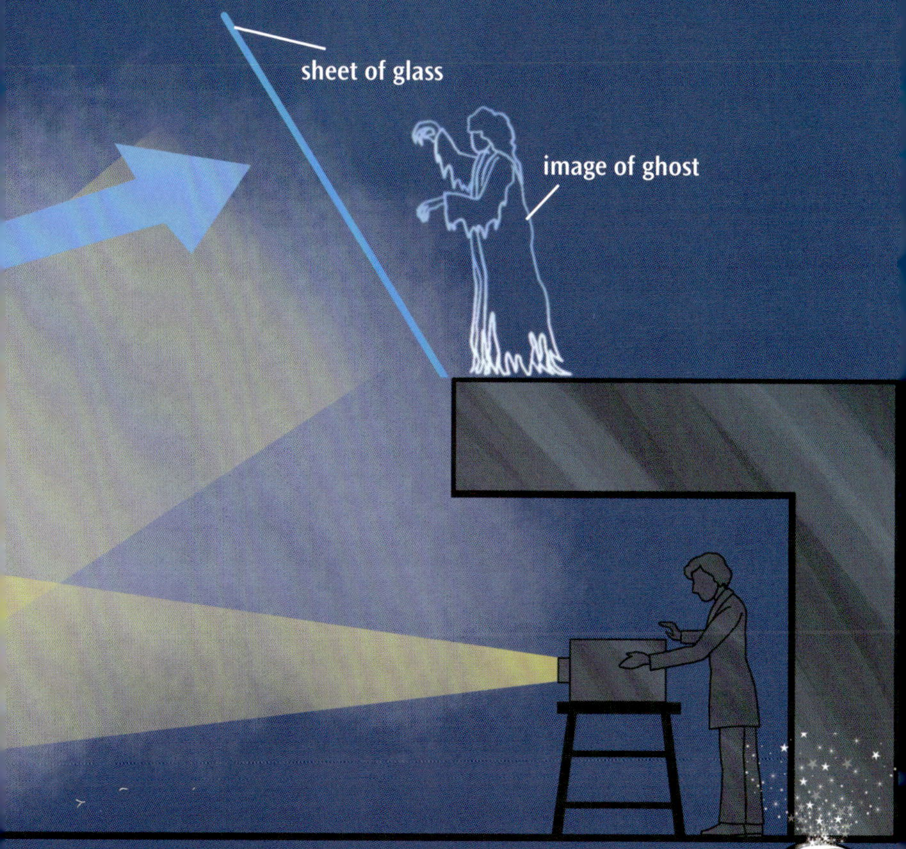

invisibility. Scientists at the University of Rochester have experimented to achieve that goal. They call their method the Rochester Cloak. Using a series of ordinary lenses, light is passed around an object. When viewed through the lenses, the object is cloaked. So, it is invisible. Any object can be cloaked with this method, but the lenses must be larger than the object for it to work well.

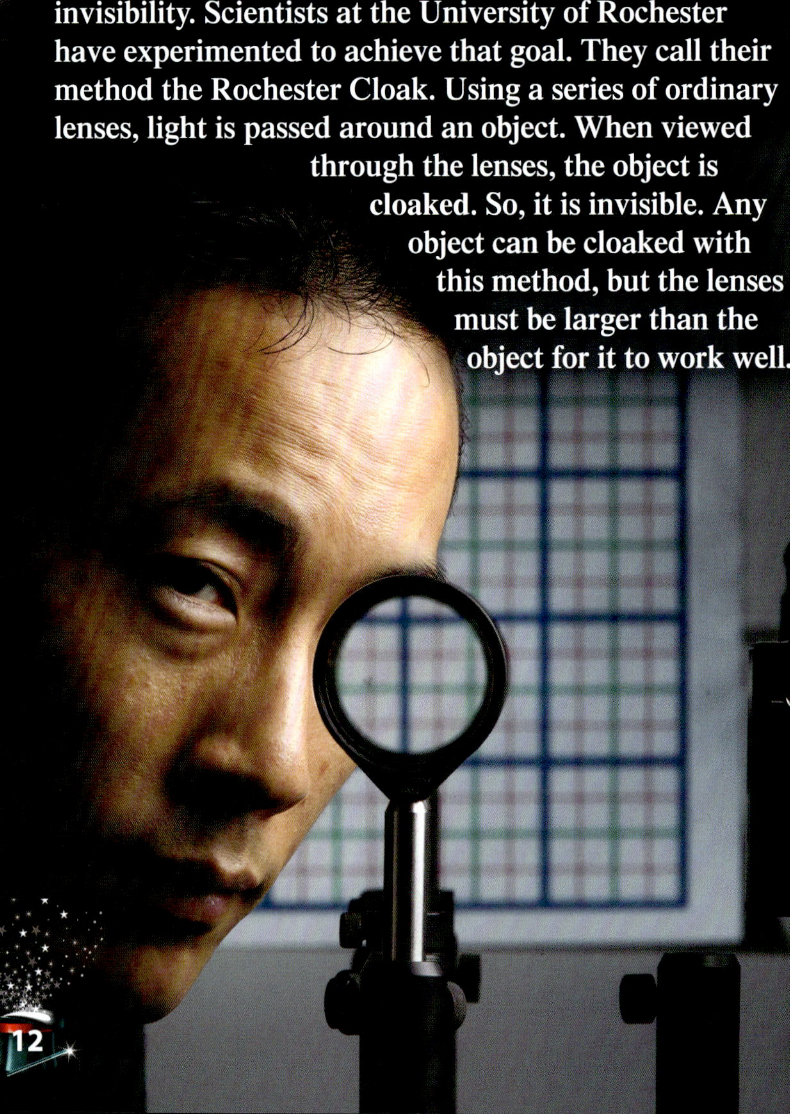

The Invisible Man

In H. G. Wells's novel, ***The Invisible Man***, a scientist discovers the secret of invisibility. He makes himself invisible but does not know how to reverse the process. This leads to disastrous consequences.

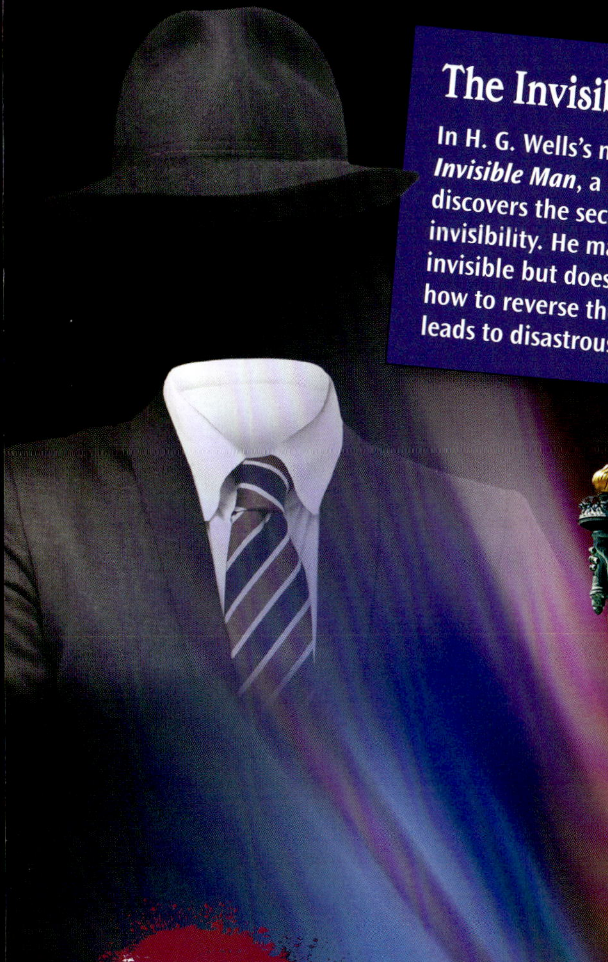

Lady Liberty Disappears

David Copperfield made the Statue of Liberty disappear on live TV in 1983. This illusion was performed at night with a live audience and camera crews. They filmed from the ground and in the air. How did he do it? Only David Copperfield and his illusion designers know for sure!

Lions, Humans, and Gold, Oh My!

In nature, transformation is part of life. Caterpillars transform into beautiful butterflies. Tadpoles transform into frogs. These natural transformations take place over long periods of time. Illusions performed by magicians, however, do not have the luxury of time. Magic shows last only an hour or two! Luckily, some great illusions have been invented that appear to defy the laws of nature in seconds flat.

The Great Lafayette performed The Lion's Bride illusion in the early 1900s. In this illusion, a lion roared and paced inside a cage. Then, a woman was put in the cage with the angry lion. The lion looked as though it was about to pounce, but then . . . pop! The head of the lion came off and Lafayette emerged. He had successfully transformed a lion into himself!

This illusion required a special cage with a false wall. Behind the wall, Lafayette waited while his helpers distracted the audience. Then, the lion was led out of the cage while Lafayette, in a realistic lion costume, took its place.

By the Light of the Moon

A werewolf is a human who transforms during a full moon into a creature that is half human and half wolf. Similar legends exist in many cultures. The human may transform into a dog or even into an animal of his/her choice.

Alchemy Transformations

Alchemists in ancient China sought an **elixir** of life that would make an old person young again. Later, alchemists in Europe looked for ways to transform a metal such as lead into gold. Neither of these transformations was accomplished or rooted in science.

Beam Me Up!

On TV and in the movies, science can do magical things. In the *Star Trek* series, characters are able to teleport from their spaceships to the surfaces of planets. But can teleportation take place in reality?

The Einstein-Rosen Bridge theory may offer some answers. Albert Einstein and Nathan Rosen created this theory in 1935. The bridge is a wormhole, or tube-like tunnel, that connects two points in space and time. Traveling through this wormhole would move you from one point to another faster than the speed of light!

Criss Angel

Teleportation on the Street

In a famous illusion on a city street, Criss Angel gathers a crowd and hands someone a walkie-talkie. A large trash can is placed over Angel, who continues to talk through the walkie-talkie. But when the trash can is lifted, Angel is gone—appearing instead on a nearby rooftop. Angel won't reveal how this is done, but maybe you can guess.

An Einstein-Rosen Bridge is not used to perform teleportation illusions. Instead, the magician directs your attention to one point while the object or person moves or is duplicated at another point. This can be done with stage props that quickly pull someone offstage. It can also be achieved through the sights, sounds, and story the magician presents. The point of view of the audience may also play a role. Only the magician knows the true method.

Monstrous Consequences

The science of teleportation takes a terrible turn in the movie *The Fly*. In it, a scientist invents a teleportation device and tests it on himself. As he gets in the machine, a fly follows him. During teleportation, the man's and fly's genes get spliced, making a man-fly hybrid!

Sleight of Hand and Misdirection

Sleight of hand! Prestidigitation! Legerdemain! These terms describe the quick and nimble handling of objects to trick the audience. Magicians can use sleight of hand to secretly remove a volunteer's watch. They can use it to produce a coin in a previously empty hand. They can even direct the audience's attention elsewhere while **deftly** switching one object for another.

Misdirection is the act of leading or directing the focus of an audience. A magician uses misdirection to control what we see. The magician also uses it to control what we won't see. Using this method with sleight of hand, a magician is able to perform secret actions outside our focus—but in plain sight of the audience.

Arcs and Straight Lines

Neuroscientists have found that when we watch an object move in a straight line, we don't follow the object. Our eyes quickly move to where we predict the object will end up. However, when an object moves in an arc, we follow the object as it moves. By misdirecting us with an arc, magicians can control where we look and perform secret actions outside our lines of sight.

The Magic of Laughter

Magicians Penn and Teller have discovered that laughter is magical. Teller remarks, "Laughter disables your ability to think critically." He goes on to explain that if he can get the audience to laugh after performing a suspicious move, the audience is less likely to remember the move.

Magician Spotlight: Ellen Armstrong

When Ellen Armstrong's father died in 1939, she took over his magic act. At the time, she was the only African American woman with her own live magic show. She performed illusions such as the Miser's Dream, in which coins appear out of thin air. The trick uses sleight of hand.

The Seven Basic Principles of Magic

Penn and Teller are a magic duo. They have been performing together since 1974. Penn is tall and talkative, while Teller is shorter and doesn't say a word during the act. Together, they have come up with the Seven Basic Principles of Magic: **palm**, **ditch**, **steal**, **load**, **simulation**, misdirection, and **switch**. Practicing sleight of hand is essential to mastering these basic principles.

Which Cup?

This sleight-of-hand trick dates back to ancient times. It starts with three cups and a ball under each cup. The cups are shuffled, and that's where the trick varies. Sometimes, the balls pass through the cups so that all three are under one cup. Sometimes, the balls transform into chicks or mice. Penn and Teller use clear cups, and the illusion still works!

Penn and Teller

In practice, a magician may *palm* an object such as a coin or ball, hiding it in his palm. He may then *ditch* that same coin or ball once it is no longer needed. The magician may then *steal* another object, such as a deck of cards, and *load* the object where it is needed in his hand. The magician may perform a *simulation* where he appears to shuffle the deck but really doesn't. Through *misdirection*, he may have the audience focus on the deck of cards in his hand while pulling a dove out of his pocket. Then, in a puff of smoke, a *switch* makes the cards disappear and the dove appear perched on the magician's hand.

All the principles may not show up in the same trick. However, at least one of the seven can be found in each trick a magician performs.

Magician Spotlight: Shin Lim

Shin Lim performs card illusions and other close-up magic around the world. Just like Teller, he remains silent during performances. He does, however, use smoke and music to set the tone. The magic speaks for itself.

DIG DEEPER!

Palming 101

Palming an object allows a magician to hide and produce an object at will. Test out your dexterity and skills of prestidigitation with these two palming techniques.

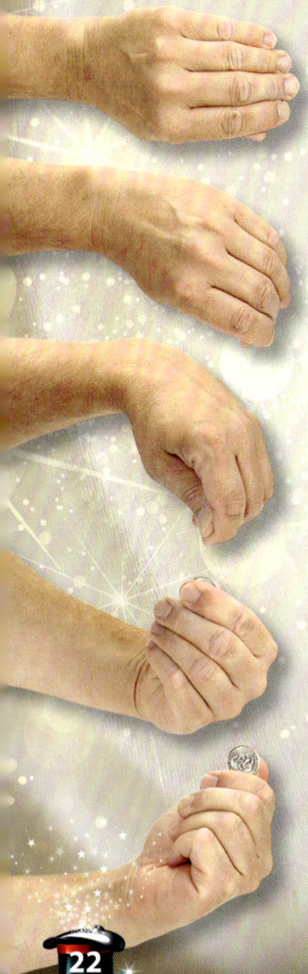

Classic Coin Palm

First, hold out your hand flat in front of you and place a coin in the center of your palm. Then, move your thumb up in the direction of your pinky. The muscles at the base of your thumb and pinky hold the coin in place. Finally, turn your hand over to test if you are really palming the coin.

Classic Card Palm

First, hold out your hand flat in front of you and place a card in your palm. Rest the bottom corner of the card against the muscle at the base of your thumb and the top corner of the card against the top section of your pinky finger. Next, apply gentle pressure with your pinky finger and the base of your thumb to grip the card. Finally, turn your hand over to test if you are really palming the card. **Tip:** Make sure that your fingers are resting together so that you cannot see the card through your fingers.

Practice, Practice, Practice

A magician's hands need to look natural while palming an object. Practice is important. Practice palming a coin or a card in front of a mirror. Keep the back of your hand to the audience (mirror) while you practice. Do your hands look natural? Is the object hidden? Once you get the move perfect for the mirror, you will be ready for a real audience.

Palming Cards 201

There are many ways to palm a card. The Tenkai Palm places the card between the thumb and palm. The card is held similarly to the coin palm position. The back palm places the card behind the palm and fingers. Instead of being *in* the hand, the card is *behind* the hand.

Profile of a Professional Pickpocket

Apollo Robbins is a professional magician and **pickpocket**. He uses sleight of hand and misdirection to **pilfer** personal items from pockets and persons. (Don't worry; he gives the items back once he is done.) He is able to do this by completely controlling a person's attention. He may unstrap and take a watch while shaking someone's hand. He may brush lightly on someone's shoulder and remove a scarf. He may step close to a volunteer and take what is inside a pants pocket, while the volunteer shows him the inside of a jacket pocket. And all this is possible by directing the spotlight of the volunteer's attention away from the theft.

Directing someone's attention is easier than you may think. It just takes some knowledge of human behavior and a little practice. To try it out, ask a friend to hold out her hand, palm facing up. Place an object such as a coin or eraser into your friend's hand. Did she look at her hand? Now, without saying anything, look at your friend's face. Did her attention move from her hand to your face?

Crime Watch!

For as long as there have been pockets there has been pickpocketing. Pickpocketing is stealing from a person's pockets without that person knowing it. It is a crime! Pickpockets may work alone or in teams to distract and confuse people.

magician Apollo Robbins

Blind to Change

Would you notice if the person you were talking to disappeared and a new person magically appeared in his or her place? If there is a visual break or a moment in which you lose visual contact with that person, maybe not. Magician and mentalist Derren Brown has conducted an experiment that tests just that.

In the experiment, Brown stops someone and asks for directions. Then, someone carrying a large object goes between Brown and the person he is talking to. For a moment, they cannot see each other. That is when the switch occurs. Brown keeps moving with the large object. And a new person steps into the conversation about directions. Do you think the people giving directions notice they are talking to someone new? The answer is no, most of the time they don't. They don't even notice when the second person looks completely different! This inability to notice large changes in our environment is called **change blindness**. It shows us just how little we take notice of and confirms why misdirection works so well.

Attention and Misdirection

A magician's secret moves go unnoticed because our attention mainly focuses on one thing at a time. This is called **inattentional blindness**. Our brains take in so much information all day long that it would be impossible to focus on everything. We focus on what is important in each moment.

Monkey Business

In one experiment on inattentional blindness conducted by Daniel Simons, an audience is asked to watch a video and count how many times a basketball is passed around a group of players. Halfway through the video a gorilla casually walks through the scene. Do the audience members notice the gorilla? Often, they don't!

Open Up Your Brain to a Mentalist

Your thoughts are not safe! Not from a mentalist, anyway. Mentalists study human behavior and psychology. They take you, the audience member, and make you and your brain part of the show. They know how the brain works and how people think. Your body language, your facial expressions, your speech, and even how you dress all give clues as to what you are thinking. Mentalists are also masters of noticing details and directing a person's thoughts through suggestion. They use words and actions to lead you to act the way they want you to.

Some mentalists claim to predict the future, and some claim they can use **psychic** powers to move matter with a concentrated stare. But it is not some supernatural or psychic power that allows them to do these things. There is always a secret move or method to their mentalism.

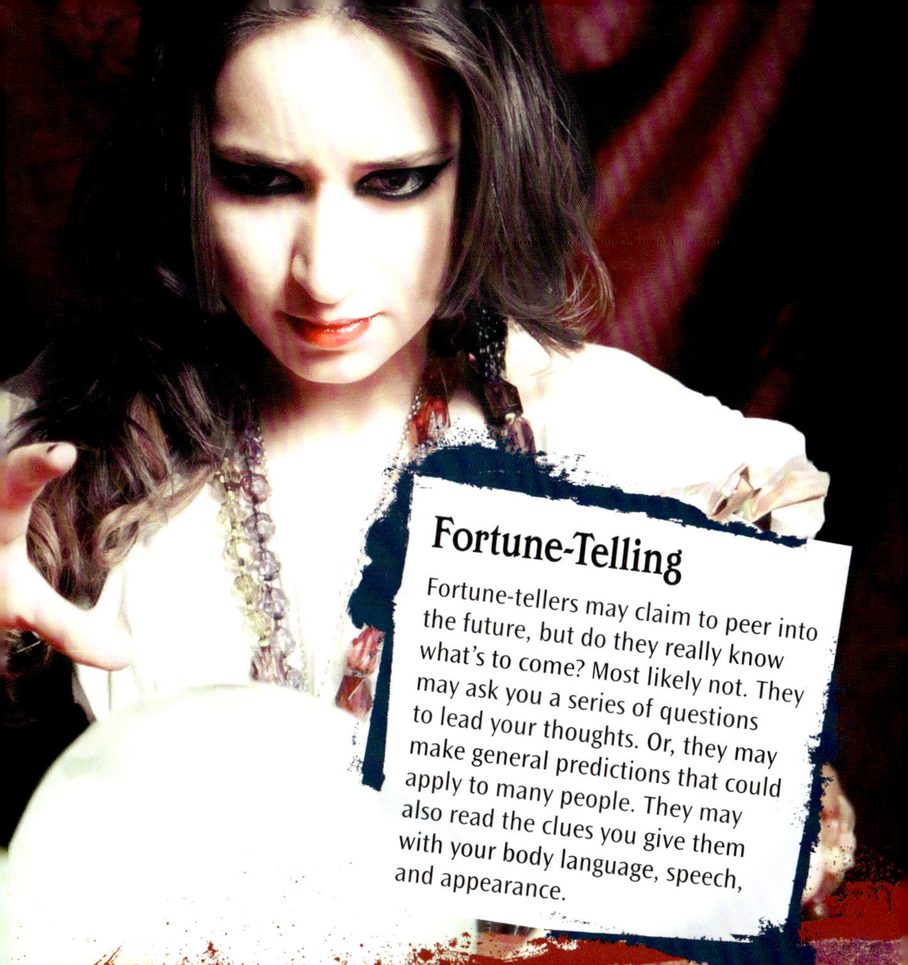

Fortune-Telling

Fortune-tellers may claim to peer into the future, but do they really know what's to come? Most likely not. They may ask you a series of questions to lead your thoughts. Or, they may make general predictions that could apply to many people. They may also read the clues you give them with your body language, speech, and appearance.

THINK LINK

Some forms of mentalism can easily be confirmed by science, while others seem more supernatural. Can you spot the difference? While reading about types of mentalism, ask yourself:

- What can be explained with science?
- What would you need to know to understand the science behind the trick?
- What topics could you research to know for sure?

Transmit Your Thoughts to Me

The art of mind reading is a favorite among mentalists and mind magicians. In some mind reading tricks, a mentalist may guess a card you are thinking of. Or blindfolded, he may call out an object that an audience member is holding up. He may also try to find an object that was hidden from him by the audience.

The Amazing Kreskin, a famous mentalist, is known for having the audience hide his paycheck for his performance. He leaves the stage while the audience hides the check. When he comes back, he chooses an audience member and asks her to think about where the check is hidden. He lightly takes hold of her hand and uses a method called **muscle reading** to lead him to his check.

The Amazing Kreskin

During muscle reading, the audience member gives subconscious clues to the direction of the object. If the object is to the volunteer's left and Kreskin moves right, there will be a slight pull of resistance in the volunteer's hand. This resistance is made subconsciously. Kreskin and other mentalists learn to read these slight movements and tremors in a person's muscles. It helps guide them to hidden objects.

The Power of Suggestion

Mentalist Derren Brown can use **subliminal messages** to lead a person's subconscious thoughts. He asks the audience to picture a card in their minds. He says, "Picture the card bright and vivid." The words "bright" and "vivid" may make you think of a red card. This works because the color black is not usually described with those terms. These types of strategies help a mentalist put an image into your mind.

The Father of Muscle Reading

The magician Axel Hellström was a master of muscle reading. He performed this feat for a group of magicians in 1928. He was so good during his demonstration that muscle reading became known as Hellströmism.

DIG DEEPER!

And the Card Is . . .

Card tricks have been performed for hundreds of years. In this trick, you will prove your skills as a mentalist by predicting the top card of a shuffled deck.

Supplies

paper, pencil, envelope, deck of cards

Set Up

1. Choose a card and withhold it from the deck.

2. Draw a picture of the card you chose, fold it, and seal it inside the envelope.

3. Place the card face down on the table in front of you so that it hangs slightly (a centimeter or so) off the table's edge. Then, place the envelope on top of the card, hiding it.

The Trick

1. Tell your audience you have made a prediction about a card in the deck and placed that card in the envelope. Ask for a volunteer who will help you magically find your predicted card within the deck.

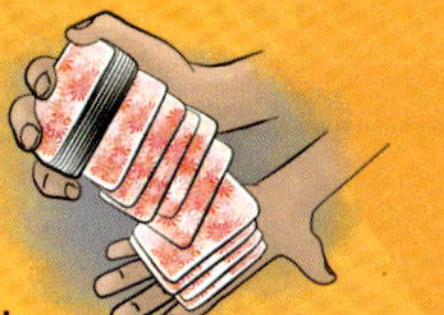

2. Give the deck of cards to the volunteer to shuffle and place into a pile on the table.

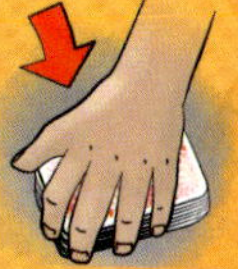

3. Once all the cards are in the pile, pick up the envelope and the card hiding beneath it and toss them on top of the pile of cards in one swift motion.

4. Tell the volunteer to open the envelope and show your drawing to the rest of the audience. Then, have the volunteer flip over the card on top of the pile, which should be the one you tossed there with the envelope.

The King of Cards

Magician Howard Thurston was known as the King of Cards. One of his most famous tricks is The Rising Cards. During this trick, audience members call for specific cards. Those called cards seem to magically rise out of a deck in Thurston's hand!

Mind Over Matter

Electrical impulses course through our brains and allow us to think and move our bodies. But do our brains have the power to control and move objects? **Psychokinesis** is the idea that we can control matter with our minds.

Many stage magicians and mentalists have used this idea to astound audiences. Some freely admit to doing this through trickery. A magician may use his breath to secretly blow a straw across a table, while moving his hand above the straw. The effect is that the power of his mind and hand are moving the straw.

EEG Diagnosis

An **electroencephalogram**, or EEG, measures and records the electrical activity in the brain. Doctors can use an EEG to view a person's brainwaves. EEGs can also detect brain abnormalities. This can help diagnose conditions such as epilepsy.

Toying with EEGs

Toy makers have found a way to simulate psychokinetic powers using an EEG headset. The headset records brain activity when a person thinks of certain commands. It then sends the commands to an object to move it—for example, a toy race car on a track!

Other entertainers have claimed to have genuine psychic abilities. They have performed tricks such as bending metal objects (e.g., spoons and keys) with their minds. However, the ability to do this has not been proven by science. Newton's First Law of Motion states that an object at rest will stay at rest unless acted upon by an unbalanced force. And there is no scientific evidence that shows the mind can generate a force great enough to move a resting object.

Lighter Than Air

Everyone has felt the pull of gravity. It is the force that keeps us on the ground and not flying into space. But, we have invented ways to overcome the pull of gravity. Airplanes, jets, and helicopters allow us to travel quickly around the world. Rockets propel us into space. Small quadcopter drones entertain us with remote-controlled fun at home.

All these examples use the forces of drag, thrust, and lift to fly. It is a balancing act of these forces that keeps a flying vehicle aloft and moving forward. As the forces of lift and thrust are increased, a vehicle moves up and forward. As they decrease, it drops in altitude and slows down. When the force of lift and the object's weight are balanced, a vehicle will fly at a constant altitude. When the force of thrust increases, it moves faster!

Daedalus and Icarus

In a Greek myth, Daedalus and his son, Icarus, escape imprisonment by flying with wings made of wax and feathers. But, Icarus flies too close to the sun and melts his wings, plummeting to Earth. Can wax wings create enough lift and thrust to carry a person? No, but it makes for an exciting story.

The Illusion of Flight

Magicians use the illusion of flying to capture our imaginations. Some illusions demonstrate a simple and controlled levitation, while other illusions may show the magician flying around the stage. In either case, magicians appear to have mastered the power of flight.

The Ethereal Suspension

The bells tolled half past eight on that Tuesday evening in 1848. It was time. The famous French **conjurer**, Robert Houdin, walked onto the stage with a walking stick and his young son in tow. "Tonight this small group of Parisians will see something new and extraordinary," Houdin thought.

A hush came over the small group watching. Houdin placed his walking stick under his son's arm like a crutch. He then produced a bottle of ether, a chemical used as an **anesthetic**. Carefully removing the cork, he walked around the stage, spilling small amounts of ether. Then, returning to his son, he ran the bottle under his son's nose. The vapors of ether slowly made his son fall asleep with his elbow leaning against the walking stick.

Everything was going to plan. Houdin's gaze pierced the audience as he gently lifted his son's legs out and up until the boy was completely parallel to the ground. Houdin then removed his hands. To the shock of the onlookers, the boy remained suspended in mid-air, peacefully leaning against the walking stick with his elbow. The **Ethereal** Suspension Illusion was born.

Chair Suspension

The Chair Suspension illusion starts with two chairs and a gurney balanced between them. A volunteer lies on the gurney. One chair is removed, and then, to the audience's amazement, the gurney is removed. The volunteer remains suspended by a hidden steel beam but appears to be held up by the back of only one chair.

Science Connection: Ether

Ether was used as an anesthetic in the 1840s. Doctors and dentists used it during surgery. When inhaled, ether vapor causes the patient to become unconscious. Houdin's audience knew of ether but probably not all its properties. They didn't know that ether cannot make a person lighter than air.

This lithograph shows Houdin's son balancing on the walking stick.

Floating in Mid-Air

Magicians are both secretive and competitive. They try to learn each other's secrets and build upon them. Many magicians built upon Houdin's Ethereal Suspension Illusion. From their work, the levitation illusion was created. In this illusion, the magician's assistant lies down on a flat surface. The magician then makes the assistant float a few feet in the air!

Each magician performs this illusion in his or her own way. The magician adds props to the illusion to make the levitation more convincing. Some magicians add metal hoops to the act. The hoops are passed around and over the floating assistants. Some magicians make the assistants disappear completely. But how do magicians make these levitations possible?

Floating on Water

In one type of floating levitation illusion, jets of water appear to lift and hold an assistant in the air. Then, the water is slowly turned off a few jets at a time and the assistant remains in the air. In reality, the assistant is being held up by a metal gurney that is hidden from view. Doug Henning and David Copperfield have incorporated this illusion into their acts.

The Invention of Magic

Magicians are also inventors. They invent props and machines to help them with their illusions. This includes strong wires that hold up floating people or machines hidden offstage that raise and lower assistants. The prop can even be as simple as a gooseneck. This is a folded metal bar that allows a magician to pass a hoop around a floating assistant.

Levitating on the Street

Self-levitation is a popular illusion that street magicians have developed. A magician moves a few feet away from the crowd, raises his arms in the air, and lifts off the ground a few inches. Magician David Blaine is one of the magicians who has made this illusion popular.

Magnetic Levitation

While stage levitations are illusions, there are some ways to levitate objects that can be backed up by science! They are done with **electromagnetism**. Think about two bar magnets. When their opposite poles are near each other, the two magnets attract. When the same poles of both magnets are near each other, they repel. And because the same poles of magnets repel each other, they can help levitate objects and make motors move.

The Linear Motor and Maglev Trains

Linear motors are used to move Maglev trains. (Maglev is short for magnetic levitation.) The motors use electromagnetism to control the movements of the trains. A linear motor pulls the train forward with the power of attraction and levitates the train above the track with the power of repulsion.

High Field Magnetic Laboratory

Researchers at Radboud University's High Field Magnetic Laboratory in the Netherlands are studying matter by creating the most powerful magnetic fields in the world. The fields are so strong that small things (for example, strawberries and frogs) placed inside the magnetic fields also become magnetized. The objects levitate within the field.

THINK LINK

- How might magnets be used for illusions in the future?
- How could magnets be used in future science and technology?
- What negative effects do you think high magnetic fields might have on the animals being used at the High Field Magnetic Laboratory?

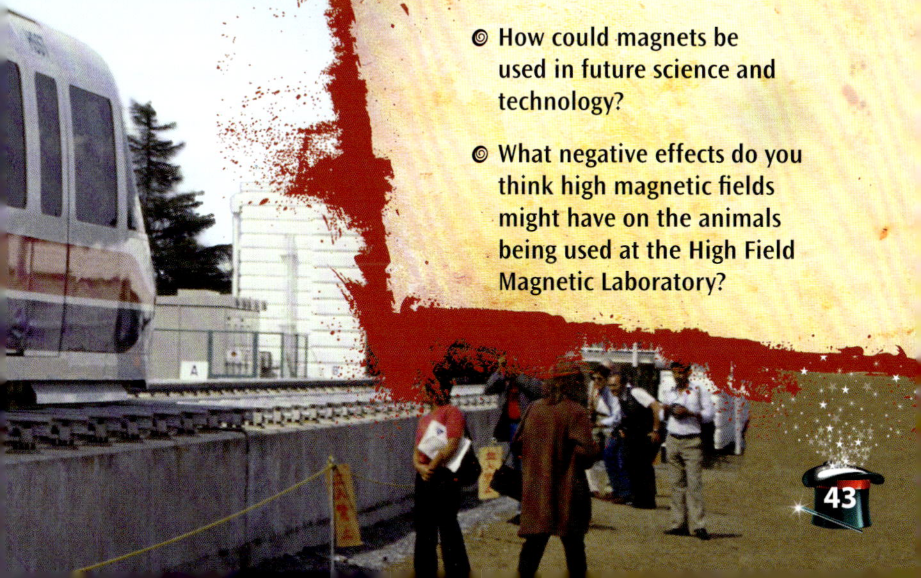

The Gift of Flight

How did magicians improve on the levitation illusion? They added the illusion of flying. Flying is a common dream many people have had throughout the ages. And today, magicians such as David Copperfield bring that dream to life.

In Copperfield's illusion, he floats off the stage and takes flight. He flies over the stage and the first few rows of the audience. He does flips in the air and moves through hoops. He flies into a glass aquarium and a lid is put on top, closing him in. Inside the closed-off aquarium, he is still able to float. Finally, a volunteer is chosen. Copperfield picks up the volunteer and carries her into the air. All these events give the audience the illusion that Copperfield is actually flying.

As with any illusion, the science is in the design and engineering of the illusion. Only Copperfield and his team of illusion designers know exactly how his flight is made possible. Some people have speculated that he uses incredibly thin and strong wires that lift him and fly him around the stage area.

Da Vinci's Flying Machine

Leonardo da Vinci is the famous artist who painted the *Mona Lisa*. But, he was also an inventor. Among da Vinci's sketches are his flying machines, including a glider. It is thought that da Vinci studied and sketched bird and bat wings in preparation for designing the glider.

Wingsuit Flying

Wingsuit flying is an extreme sport that is similar to skydiving and BASE jumping. The suits have inflatable nylon cells that increase the surface area of the flyer. This gives the flyer greater lift and, in turn, the increased lift slows the flyer's descent and allows the flyer to stay in the air.

Daring Physical Feats

A magician shackled in chains jumps from a bridge into a river. How will he escape from his bonds? How long can he hold his breath before he drowns? Another magician adeptly swallows a sword. How is she not cut up inside? A magician traps himself in ice. How cold can a body get before suffering from hypothermia? Still, another magician sets a deck of cards aflame or extinguishes a fire by eating it. How does the magician control the fire and not get burned?

In all these performances, the magicians test the physical limits of their bodies. The magicians also challenge what we think we know about the science of the human body. There is an element of danger involved with any trick of this nature. Magicians must learn all they can about their own bodies and the elements they use in the illusions, so they can stay safe while still astounding us.

Warning! Do Not Try This at Home

The magic tricks and illusions presented in this chapter are dangerous. They are so dangerous, in fact, that many people have become seriously injured and have died in practicing and performing these acts. Do not try, or even think about trying, any of the performances you are about to read.

Trapped in Ice

David Blaine is a magician who continually pushes the limits of his body. In 2000, Blaine trapped himself in a five-ton block of ice for nearly 64 hours! Normally, such long exposure to ice would result in hypothermia. As a person's body temperature dips below 95 degrees Fahrenheit (35 degrees Celsius), the heart rate slows and the body cannot function normally. Cells and tissue can begin to die. Blaine completed the challenge unharmed.

Harry Houdini is one of the most famous escape artists of all time. His performances were followed closely by people in the media. He even offered rewards to anyone who successfully built handcuffs that could restrain him!

Houdini Escapes Water Torture Cell!

Berlin, Germany, September 21, 1912—Harry Houdini, the greatest escape artist of our time, has topped himself once again! Dead silence was all that could be heard at the Circus Busch this Saturday night as wooden stocks were placed around the ankles of the King of Handcuffs. All were captivated as he was raised into the air above a glass tank of water and dropped in, headfirst. Trapped inside the tank of water upside down, Houdini thrashed. His assistants quickly pulled curtains around the tank as the crowd waited in anticipation. Moments later, Houdini popped out from behind the curtain, wet from head to toe. The audience erupted in applause. What a sight to behold!

Classified Ad: Challenge to Houdini

I know many have challenged you before. And you have successfully escaped time and time again. You are, of course, the so-called King of Handcuffs. But, you will never be able to escape *my* handcuffs. They will hold your wrists so tightly, that not even *you* will be able to wiggle free. I will pay you 1,000 marks if you can escape them. Meet me outside Circus Busch this Tuesday, September 24, if you dare.

Jail Break

Houdini was once challenged to break out of an unescapable jail cell in Washington, D.C. He escaped in around two minutes. To the warden's surprise, while escaping, he also let out the other prisoners and locked them up in different cells.

A History of Escape

Houdini didn't become a master of escape overnight. Starting out, he practiced learning how to slip out of rope knots and unlock handcuffs. He studied different types of locks and how to unlock them. He even served as an apprentice to a locksmith to strengthen his skills.

All of his practice and hard work paid off, and Houdini could escape any lock or any restraint presented to him. He could escape handcuffs with no available key. He could break out of prison cells and escape chains and padlocks, even while sinking into the depths of New York City's East River. He challenged the public to present him with restraints he could not escape.

One popular illusion for which Houdini was known was called the Metamorphosis. In this illusion, Houdini was bound with rope and put in a sack, which was then put in a trunk. An assistant would pull a curtain around himself and the trunk. The assistant clapped three times, and the curtain was drawn to reveal Houdini. Houdini then opened the trunk to reveal his assistant, bound and inside the sack!

Don't Hold Your Breath!

Stig Severinsen holds the Guinness World Record for holding his breath. In 2012, he held it underwater for 22 minutes. Stig hyperventilated with pure oxygen before submerging into the water. This breathing technique saturated his blood with oxygen and allowed him to stay under longer! Definitely don't try this yourself!

That's So Metal!

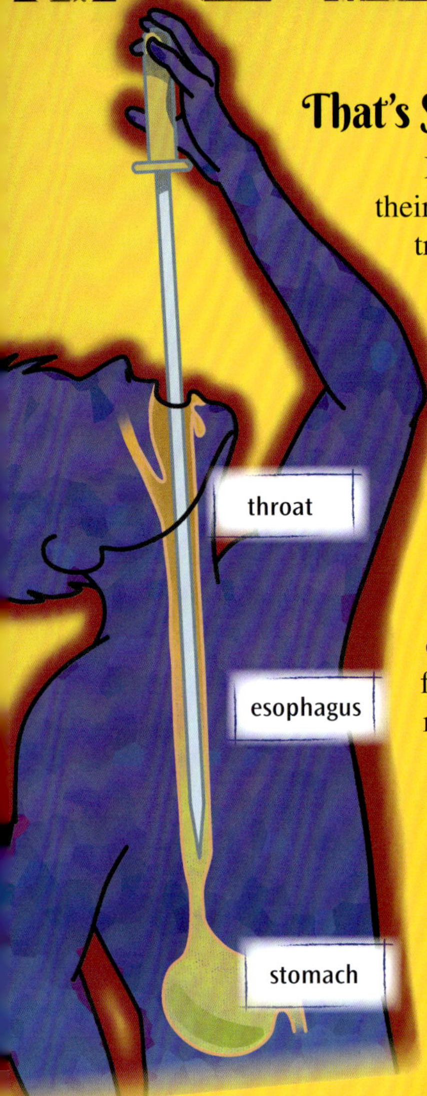

Magicians can be fearless. Some risk their lives to entertain. This is especially true with sword swallowing. During a sword-swallowing performance, a magician tilts his head back and carefully slides a sword down his throat, past his esophagus, and into his stomach. How is this possible?

Even though it is called sword swallowing, the magician is not swallowing the sword. It is the exact opposite in fact. When we swallow food, we use the soft tissue and muscles in our throats and esophagus to carry it to our stomachs. With sword swallowing, the magician must completely relax and stop those muscles from contracting. He must have complete control over his body. One muscle twitch or gag reflex and the magician could be fatally wounded. To make things even more dangerous, the sword passes by many vital organs on the way to the stomach, including the heart. One slip of the blade and the esophagus, stomach, or even the heart can be punctured.

Controlling the body's reflexes takes great skill and practice. Many amateur sword swallowers have become injured or even died!

Needle Swallowing

One of Harry Houdini's famous tricks was needle swallowing. He would appear to swallow dozens of sewing needles. Just as quickly, he would then swallow thread. Holding one end of the thread, Houdini would pull the thread from his mouth—with all the needles perfectly threaded on the string!

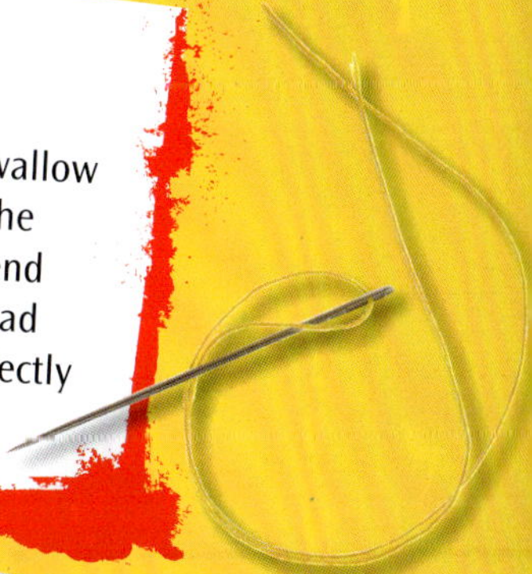

STOP! THINK...

- What are the health risks involved with sword swallowing?
- Some sword swallowers use wavy or curved blades. How do you think they are able to swallow these swords?
- How could people make sword swallowing a safe endeavor?

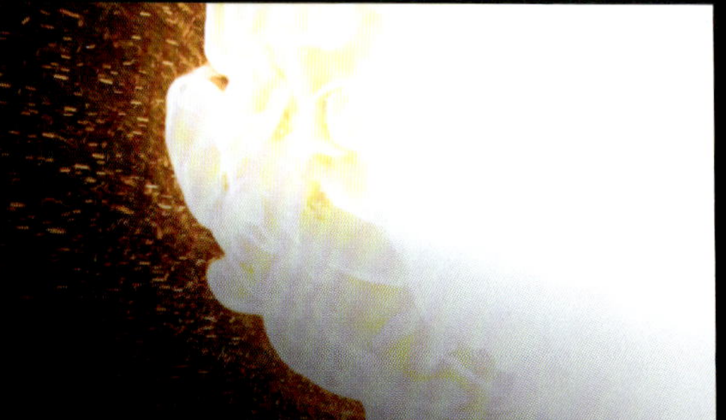

Fire Up the Magic

When you think of magic and fire, you might think of dragons. But there is something magical about fire on its own. Fire is wild and destroys everything it touches, but it is also bright and captivating. Magicians use fire to draw attention. They may catch a card on fire, or they may even breathe fire like dragons themselves.

Fire is the result of a chemical reaction, called combustion, between a fuel source and oxygen. When a fuel source heats up to ignition temperature, it combusts. The fire remains burning until the fuel is used up or there is no oxygen.

Knowing the science behind fire allows magicians to work more safely with fire in their acts. Whether creating a small fireball in their hand or igniting an object, magicians can control the conditions of the fire. This means they can control the amount of time the object burns and the visual impact it has.

Fire Breathing

Two ingredients are needed to create the illusion of breathing fire: fuel and a fire source. The fuel used is usually a special type of flammable liquid with low **volatility**. This lowers the risk of the fire flaming back into the breather's face.

Is Magic Real?

Magicians use science and technology to fool our senses. They create illusions that trick our eyes and use sleight of hand to dupe our brains. They invent stage props that make the impossible look possible.

Humans don't understand everything about the known universe. Science allows us to study things we don't understand, things that may appear magical. And over time, we sometimes come to understand how the magic works—and it becomes science. Think of modern inventions such as airplanes, computers, or even the common household light bulb. At one time, all these would have been considered magical.

So, does real magic exist? Maybe it is just a matter of perspective. Remember, what seems like magic today may be the science of tomorrow.

Magician Spotlight: Megan Knowles-Bacon

Megan Knowles-Bacon puts on a unique show. She incorporates ballet moves into her magic routine! In 2014, Megan was elected to an officer role in the Magic Circle Society in London. At 22, she became the youngest person and first woman to be elected to such a position.

THINK LINK

- What are some things that seem magical today that may prove to be the science of tomorrow?
- What are some other examples of science that at one time were considered magic?
- Do you think that magic is real? Why or why not?

Megan Knowles-Bacon performs her magic.

Glossary

anesthetic—a drug that causes loss of feeling or ability to feel pain

change blindness—the inability to notice large changes in the environment

cloaked—hidden or invisible

conjurer—a magician or performer of tricks

deftly—skillfully

ditch—to get rid of an unneeded object

electroencephalogram (ih-lek-troh-in-SEF-uh-luh-gram)—a test that uses a machine to measure and record the electrical activity in the brain

electromagnetism—a magnetic field produced by an electric current

elixir—a magical healing liquid

ethereal—delicate and heaven like

illusions—deceptions; things that appear real but aren't

inattentional blindness—the inability to notice actions outside of our focus of attention

levitations—rising or lifting things to float

load—to place an object where it is needed

mentalist—a mind reader; someone who practices mind magic

misdirection—to direct attention away from a secret move

muscle reading—to read subtle muscle movements in a subject

palm—to hide an object in the palm of your hand

patter—the story; a prepared script to lead the audience

pickpocket—a person who steals from people's pockets

pilfer—to steal stealthily

psychic—having supernatural mental powers

psychokinesis—the ability to control matter with the mind

simulation—to pretend to do something

sleight of hand—a quick and nimble hand movement; prestidigitation; legerdemain

specter—ghost

steal—to obtain an object that doesn't belong to you

subliminal messages—information and messages that are retained by the subconscious

supernatural—something that is beyond the laws of nature

switch—to change one object for another

teleportations—instantaneous movements of objects from one place to another

transformations—changes that occur when one thing changes into another

volatility—likely to change suddenly

Index

Check It Out!

Books

DK. 2014. *Children's Book of Magic*. DK Children.

Eldin, Peter. 1997. *Magic*. Kingfisher.

Fleischman, Sid. 2006. *Escape: The Story of the Great Houdini*. Greenwillow Books.

Jay, Joshua. 2014. *Big Magic for Little Hands*. Workman Publishing Company.

Randi, James. 1989. **The Magic World of the Amazing Randi**. Adams Media Corporation.

Schafer, Albert D. 2012. Illusionology: *The Secret Science of Magic*. Candlewick Press.

Videos

BBC. 2004. *Magic (MiniSeries)*. British Broadcasting Corporation.

Don Herbert. 1985. *Mr. Wizard's World (Season 3 Ep. 1)*. Music Television/Nickelodeon.

Websites

American Museum of Magic. http://www.americanmuseumofmagic.org/.

Try It!

Imagine that you have been transported back in time. The people in the village see you standing there in your strange clothes and think you must be a wizard! So, you decide to amaze them with a magic trick.

- Write a short story or memoir by hand or on a computer. Include illustrations or diagrams that might help explain your appearance to the villagers.
- What time period will you travel to? Research details from that era.
- Once you've gathered your research, describe which trick you will perform.
- You're wearing a jacket with many pockets on this journey. What might you have brought to help you perform your "magic"?

About the Author

James Anderson grew up in Orange County, California. His fascination with magic began when he was given a book of magic tricks for his tenth birthday. James realized quickly that what he enjoyed most about magic was understanding how the magic tricks work. His favorite types of magic involve sleight of hand. He always watches closely to see if he can spot the secret moves.